How to Get a Job in 24 Hours

- Not just any job, but the job you want
- This unique approach can make it possible
- Proven to work with astonishing results

Jas Gates

authorHOUSE®

AuthorHouse™
1663 Liberty Drive, Suite 200
Bloomington, IN 47403
www.authorhouse.com
Phone: 1-800-839-8640

First published by AuthorHouse 8/25/2008

ISBN: 978-1-4343-1639-4 (sc)

Printed in the United States of America
Bloomington, Indiana

This book is printed on acid-free paper.

Acknowledgements

Thanks to the following:

John Dillon and Paul Gudgeon for their feedback on the initial draft.

Edwige for her assessment and contribution and D. Phuangpho for her consistent encouragement.

My editor, Sharon R. Emeigh for her dedication and her perseverance.

I would also like to thank AuthorHouse for all their hard work.

This book is dedicated to all those who have assisted me during my years of research in this field.

About the Author

Jas Gates is a Computer Studies graduate with a wide range of experience in sales and marketing. He currently works as a Freelance Job Coach and IT Consultant in London and runs his own internet business. He is a commendable member of the Kamon Martial Arts Federation, and plans to get more involved in promoting the substantial benefits that can be gained from practising the art.

After many years researching different employers' interview strategies, Jas developed an approach to job hunting that has been continuously tried, tested and refined.

Over the years, Jas has helped hundreds to improve their job interview techniques through seminars and one-to-one tuition.

Jas believes that looking for a job can be a pleasurable experience, and much easier than we might think.

By using the easy to follow techniques outlined in this book, you will undoubtedly learn for yourself how to get the job you want in 24 hours. The inevitable fast results will change your perspective towards job hunting forever.

Contents

1. Introduction

During your job search it is essential to keep an open mind and to react positively to any obstacles you may be confronted with. With persistence you will get the job you want.

Though most of us think that it is virtually impossible to get a good job in 24 hours, these pages will explain how you can do it. Even if you are already familiar with some of the techniques and strategies described, you can use this book to complement your existing job hunting procedures.

Start off by asking yourself the following questions:

Which job do I ultimately want?
Which jobs must I do to get the job I ultimately want?

You need to know where you're heading in order to be sure that you reach your destination. Whether you are a recent graduate, have found it difficult to get work, are trying to break into a new field of work or have been made redundant, this book is for you.

Job hunting doesn't have to be a full-time engagement, just well organised and focused. Having conducted a substantial amount of research, the results I found amazed me, and I'd like to share this knowledge with you.

After reading this book, your views on job hunting will fall close to the following statement:

The task of finding a job is a rather simple one.

Once you have learned to adopt the techniques described in this book, you may well become over-confident. Giving this impression is seldom interpreted negatively.

Allow me to introduce Jack: Jack is different from the average job-seeker. His success rate in passing job interviews is around 80%, and his success rate in obtaining employment in a suitable position within 24 hours is 50%. Not bad, don't you think?

After reading the following pages you will be in a position to believe it can be done.

Don't approach this book with skepticism; give it a go and be sure of yourself. Keep an open mind and you will undoubtedly see astonishing results.

Please note:
Although this book teaches you on how to get a job in just 24 hours, it will take you about 2 weeks to master these techniques. Therefore, give yourself some leeway. It's always better to allow more time for preparation than is needed. In other words, don't limit yourself with 24 hours to find a job until you are ready.

2. The Way We Think

Not all of us think in the same way; people have different personalities. But anyone, regardless of background, may gain from these principles in one way or another. The job- hunting procedures covered throughout this book can be adapted to suit both you and your potential employers' needs. So long as one doesn't deviate too far from the methodology, a successful job search is inevitable.

It is important to learn how to use the energy needed in your job search. Positive thoughts will create productivity, whereas blaming, criticising or arguing with people are negative ways of utilising energy. Instead, whenever a problem arises, deal with it rather than pointing the finger. Avoid harsh self-appraisals - the damage has been done - look to the future and learn from the experience. The important thing is to learn from past mistakes in order to avoid repeating them in the future. You don't need to feel disillusioned or ashamed of yourself for having made a mistake; none of us are perfect, after all.

In the same way that people have different personalities, there are also different attitudes to work that one can learn from. In Japan, for instance, there is a very high-disciplined attitude towards work. Japanese workers seldom miss project deadlines. Unfinished work is finished outside of office hours, and if a project is completed early, the next one is quickly started. Adopting this attitude will give the impression that you are an efficient and dedicated worker. After all, it's not necessarily overtime workers who are rewarded with promotions, but those who are well organized and productive. However, it is important to remember to have a good work/life balance.

If you believe in luck, pretend not to. If you choose to believe in luck, then the logical conclusion is that one has to be lucky to succeed. For those that don't, it's only a matter of time before they achieve their success. Jack, generally didn't believe in luck, but if he had the tendency to do so, he would act as if he was one of the luckiest people around. As an indirect result, he received numerous job offers.

Jack knew he was successful in finding employment, so he wanted to help others and decided to place an advert in his local paper:

Job Hunting?
For expert advice contact a professional!
Tel: 020 XXXX XXXX
Email: jack707@hotmail.com

A few days later he received a call, and arranged to meet his first student: Maria.

Maria: So do you have a job for me?
Jack: No, but I do offer expert advice.
Maria: Great! I don't seem to have any luck in job interviews, what advice are you able to give me?
Jack: Putting it in a nutshell, you just need to know how to answer the following two questions:
How will the company benefit from you?
How will you benefit from the company?
Maria: Oh, I know all this already. Thanks anyway.

Maria's attitude was flippant, but is not an uncommon one among job seekers. Although she thought she knew the answers to Jack's two questions, had she really been confident in her answers to these questions she would have been more successful in her interviews. Give these two questions a lot of attention; they are the key to your success and confidence in job hunting.

The way you think determines your success. If you think it's easy to become successful in your job search, or even make-believe that it is easy, it may well become so. Believe you deserve more than the average person and you will achieve more than the average person. Looking for a job can be a pain or it can be a pleasurable experience; it depends upon the manner in which you perceive the task of job hunting.

3. Goal Setting

Job hunting can take as little as a day; or, it can take a week, several weeks or even several months. It all depends on how you think, what you expect, and the procedures you use. It will obviously take longer to get a job where the employer's recruitment procedures tend to be lengthier. E.g., a qualified nurse seeking employment in the public sector will have to go through all the appropriate channels. You might then ask yourself if it is possible for her to get a job in 24 hours. Where recruitment procedures are strict, after reading this book, you will learn how to substantially speed up the recruitment process.

It is important to set goals because doing so speeds up processes. Make a list of tasks that need to be completed in order for your goal to be achieved. A goal set by a pessimist might be something like 'This month I will arrange three interviews and just maybe I'll succeed in one of them'. An optimist might plan to pass all three interviews and within a shorter timeframe.

However, ensure that the goals you set are achievable; goals must be realistic. How does one define whether a goal is realistic or not? Well, if a goal is possible to achieve then it is achievable within a given timeframe. Goals just beyond reach enable you to tap into more of your potential. Maintain a positive attitude; do not allow any rejection you encounter along the way to affect your confidence.

Imagine the following scenario:
Two fishermen, Fred and Tom, fish in different ponds. Fred fishes in Pond A, while Tom fishes in Pond B. Now let's suppose that in Pond A there are very few fish, whereas Pond B is positively heaving with them. Which fisherman will catch more fish by the end of the day?

Instinctively, your answer would be Tom, as Pond B contains more fish. Realistically though, however, there is a tendency to relax when one has so much choice. As Fred knows that it will be difficult to catch the fish, his attempts are much more determined and consistent. Tom, however, knowing that the odds are in his favor, may take a more relaxed approach and slack after catching his first few fish. Therefore, Fred may end up catching a greater number of fish.

Let's now suppose that Fred and Tom are job hunters and the ponds are areas containing companies; Fred's area doesn't have many companies, whereas Tom's is saturated with them. The same argument can apply in this scenario: by being focused in his job hunting Fred could be more successful than Tom. If, on the other hand, Tom had set a goal to catch x number of fish, this would minimize any tendency to slack. A positive attitude and determined approach can reap rewards even if the market seems to be against you.

Clear goals and objectives are required for an effective job search, and knowing the kind of work you are looking for will keep it in focus. No one is really looking for 'anything'. Without clear job search goals the search will not be as effective. Here is an example of the approach of somebody who really wasn't sure what he wanted:

'I am not sure which type of work I really want, but I am confident that some of my skills would be useful in at least one of your departments.'

Yet, if said with confidence, it would actually reflect your belief in your own ability rather than your confusion.

Here is an example of a statement given from someone who knows what she wants but perhaps doesn't qualify for the position. (She may not be very good at the job because she lacks the knowledge and experience, but she is a keen learner):

'I would be interested in any position in your purchasing department that would enable me to utilise more of my skills. Even a junior position would make it worthwhile for me; as I believe my skills are needed in this environment.'

Setting out a logic flow diagram helps to visualise your goals. Here is an example:

<u>Step 1</u>
Start
'Are you smart and intelligent?'
 If 'yes', then go to step 2.
 If 'no', then return to step 1.

<u>Step 2</u>
'Are you confident?'
 If 'yes', then go to step 3.
 If 'no', then return to step 1.

<u>Step 3</u>
Goal
'I will get a job in 24 hours.'

Believe you are smart and intelligent and you will progress to step 2.
Believe in your own confidence and this will allow you to get the job
you want fast.

4. Learn To Sell Yourself

The marketing of a product is every bit as important as its quality. Often enough, products will not sell themselves, and so it must fall to a salesperson. Moreover, if a salesperson is good, he can probably sell anything. He may not even need to have substantial product knowledge; he can sell just by concentrating on the benefits of the product. Take, for example, a car salesman; he doesn't need to know the way the car engine works, but simply the fact that it has electric windows, ample leg room, and has a certain engine size, etc. Just by knowing and communicating the desirable features will convince a customer.

I'm sure you know more about yourself than the average car salesman does about a car. Then, shouldn't it be easier for you to sell yourself (to an employer) than to sell a car, or anything else for that matter? Whatever personality type you fall in, i.e. whether you are an extrovert or introvert, we all have the potential to sell. Once you know how to sell yourself, the words 'unemployed', 'but', 'I cannot', and any other negative phrases that you can think of, will no longer have a place in your vocabulary during your job search.

Selling yourself does not necessarily involve complete disclosure; after all, an over-honest salesman may end up having zero sales. For example, if a sales assistant told a customer who was interested in a flower vase that it was easily broken, then the customer would quickly lose interest in the vase. And yet you don't have to be dishonest to sell. Successful salesmanship evolves from a focus on the positive.

If the technology is available to you, record a video of yourself. You are an actor and you have just one scene: the interview. Learn to master it. Practice at sounding confident and talented. While you don't have to go to drama school to learn to act positively in job interviews, investing in a few 'rehearsals' will be exceptionally rewarding. If you are desperate for a job, learn the technique of concealing your nerves and anxieties.

A significant number of recent graduates I spoke with told me that the reason they went on to postgraduate studies was due to their failure in obtaining full-time employment in their original field. To get a job is a skill in itself; no wonder many people find it difficult. They simply haven't given themselves the opportunity of acquiring this skill.

Assume that everything is negotiable! Recruitment policies are sure to be updated from time to time. Whether they are written or verbal, don't let them put you at a disadvantage. There is no harm in attempting to bend these policies even if you could be the first person to attempt it.

Aim to be 100% positive. Consider the following scenario:

Jack walked into a fashion store to look for a jacket. As he browsed through the stock, a sales assistant headed towards him.

Sales assistant: Hi, are you looking for anything in particular?
Jack: No, not really.
Sales assistant: Would you like to try this jacket on?
Jack: Why not! (Jack stands in front of a mirror and tries on the jacket). How does it look?
Sales assistant: Excellent! The fit is perfect, it really suits you.
Jack: I'll take it.

A different attitude from the sales assistant would lead to the following scenario:

Jack: How does it look?
Sales assistant: It looks ok, but maybe the collar is a bit too short or the sleeves are too long.
Jack: I'll leave it. Thanks anyway.

In the second situation, the sales assistant focused on reasons why Jack shouldn't buy the jacket. The sales assistant is selling the jacket to Jack in the same way a job applicant might sell himself to the employer. By saying just one negative thing in an interview, you run the risk of the interviewer focusing on that when it comes to making a decision. Learn to linger on the positive. In a job interview it's actually better to be overconfident than lacking in assurance. Indeed, somebody somewhere might even perceive you as being a genius!

5. Analysis of the Employer's Requirements

The process of examining and understanding the requirements of an employer is important. Analyse the job description by picking out both the essential skills and desirable skills, and establish what the employer is looking for. Then you can deduce how to adapt your interview presentation to best meet the employer's needs. For example, a person with a background in psychology applying for a position as an office manager would not talk too much about his experience in psychology, but would instead focus on skills and interests that are relevant to the position applied for.

Match your qualifications to the perceived requirements of the potential job opening. A good approach is to write out your qualifications alongside the requirements.

Jack was told at an interview that his experience in Internet Security was limited. Here is how he tackled this:

'I agree with you, my experience in Internet Security is limited, but

1 – I am a fast learner.
2 – Time is money. I analysed the job description prior to being interviewed. If there was any doubt in my mind that this position was not one I would be suitable for, then I wouldn't have applied for the opening.
3 – I am (or will be) enhancing my knowledge within this area within the next one to two weeks'.

Also, acknowledge your own requirements. You don't have to be willing to take any job temporarily if it is not the one that you really want. You have a choice. Target the job that you want or at least the industry you want to work in.

One of my former students set a goal to work for a major airline as an airline hostess. She didn't settle for second best. She put all her time and effort into making her dream come true. By analysing the job description, she had the upper hand in communicating just how she would fulfill the requirements.

Consider the following Job Advertisement:

Security Officer Wanted
-To join our patrol team at one of London's top casinos.
-You should be comfortable with standing for long periods at a time, often outside.
-You should be well presented, with superb spoken English.
Email jobs@xxxxx.co.uk.

By analysing this advert, it can be deduced that the requirements needed for this position are:
Experience in security
A Team player
Physically fit
Smartly presentable
Well-spoken

Your next step towards getting this job is to communicate to the employer that you have more than the adequate requirements for this position. Giving examples of situations where you have used these required skills will score you points.

6. Your Skills

Identifying your skills is essential to your job search. Employers want to know what you can do for them, not simply what you have done for someone else. Knowledge of your own skills is needed to successfully complete an application, write a curriculum vitae or answer interview questions, and yet most people can identify only a few of their skills. Ask those who know you well, and you will see that you have skills you may not have been aware of.

Employers need to hear what you can do. If you can't articulate your skills, then they won't give you the opportunity to display them. You are a product that would cost thousands of pounds a year for many years. From this perspective, it is obvious that your strengths and abilities must be known. You are not ready to even begin approaching employers until you can clearly tell them what you can do.

Jack's skills include the following:

Time management, organisational ability, a reasonable typing speed, negotiating and debating skills, effective communication, a good presentation technique, computer graphics know-how, can speak basic mandarin, minute taking, teaching skills, and creative writing.

Although having key skills is what the interviewer may well focus on, generally, the more skills you can be seen as having, the better. This is because you may have an essential or desirable skill that wasn't mentioned in the job description.

For example, Jack applies to a company that requires someone with creative writing skills. Among Jack's skills is his ability to speak basic Mandarin. The employer suddenly remembers that the company will be expanding to China and quickly realizes that Jack's ability to speak Mandarin would be a huge benefit.

Later on I will introduce the Attribute-Advantage Table, which can be used to analyse your skills and deduce how each skill can be beneficial in the position applied for.

7. Generating Leads

Generating leads is a crucial step towards securing your ideal job. In business, it takes just one phone call to initiate and subsequently establish a professional relationship. The telephone is a powerful ally in the job search, and the initial contact made by telephone is a useful foot in the door.

Find a list of businesses that specialise in, or have a department that is relevant to your field. The Internet is a great resource, as it has a number of online business directories. Some of these give detailed information on companies, such as the number of employees, annual turnover, and the names of the directors. A list of 30 companies is a good start. Obviously, the more leads you can get, the more opportunities you will generate for yourself.

Compile the following details for each company:

- *Company name*
- *Address*
- *Website*
- *Contact name*
- *Telephone number*
- *Email address*
- *Notes*

(Use the 'Notes' section to compile information about the company that may be useful later, e.g., know that they trade internationally if you are a linguist or that they are web based if you have internet skills.)

It's what you know and whom you know! The question you might ask yourself is: *How long does it take to get to know someone?* Building a rapport with your initial contact in a company is important. Aim to build a rapport with this initial contact within two minutes of telephone conversation. In order to achieve this, it is important that you develop your telephone skills. There are plenty of resources on the web to help you with your telephone techniques. Basic telesales skills will work as a catalyst towards achieving your goal of employment.

Once a contact has been established, maintain it so that a professional relationship can develop. Or, if you have had a problem building a rapport, then anticipate this potential hiccup next time you call. By adding the personal touch in your communication, you can improve your success rate.

Consider the following telephone conversation:

Jack: Hello. Good morning! Mr. Jacobs, please.
PA: Mr. Jacobs is busy at the moment. I'm his personal assistant. How can I help?
Jack: Its Jack, here. I'm calling to find out about any possible openings your company might have in the future. Your name is?
PA: Sally.
Jack: I really do need to speak with him and I need just a couple of minutes of his time. When do you suggest I call back?
PA: He's pretty much tied up all day.
Jack: Okay. I'll call back again. Thank you for your time, Sally.

The next day:

Jack: Hello. Good morning. Is that Sally?
Sally: Yes. Who is this?
Jack: Good morning Sally. It's Jack, here. We spoke yesterday. How are you today?
Sally: Fine, thank you.
Jack: Is Mr. Jacobs available?
Sally: I'll just transfer you.

The friendly approach can be more effective than the persuasive approach. Sometimes, however, you may have to be a little persuasive in order to get the receptionist or PA to put your call through to the essential contact. Remember you are a salesperson and persuasive salespeople can succeed.

Whether your list of leads includes contact names or not, you should call the company to confirm that the contact is still available.

Here is another example:

Jack: Good morning. May I know the name of the person responsible for recruiting new programmers in your IT department?
Secretary: Who are you?
Jack: My name is Jack Smith. I looked up your number from your website and I'd like to send in my details. To whom should I address them?
Secretary: Address them to the IT manager.
Jack: And who would that be?
Secretary: John Taylor
Jack: Thanks. May I confirm the address? I've got down 4X Pine Street, London WC1XXX.
Secretary: Right.
Jack: And you are?
Secretary: Liz.
Jack: Thank you, Liz. You've been a great help.

8. The Telephone Is Your Greatest Tool In Your Job Search

Once you have established your list of contacts, the next step is to have a conversation with each of your contacts. The conversation must be a two-way dialogue and both parties must feel that the conversation was of mutual benefit.

Bottom-Up approach
This approach is used when one asks for the name of someone in the company at a lower management level, e.g. the recruitment coordinator or personal assistant. In some companies the managing director's personal assistant tends to be more involved in the communication with the company's business affairs than the managing director. The personal assistant could be the one in the office most of the time taking calls, writing emails, etc., so he or she knows the precise status of the business.

Top-Down approach
This is the approach used when targeting someone in middle or senior management. With smaller companies it is usually the managing director or owner who makes the ultimate decisions, but with larger companies the decision-maker could be someone in middle or lower management. If you feel reluctant to speak to a director, you will find (as with a lot of things) that it gets easier with practice.

The Top-Down approach can be more effective, as illustrated in the next example:

Jack: May I know the name of the managing director of the company?
Receptionist: Her name is Amy Brown.
Jack: Is she available?
Receptionist: I'll just transfer you.

Amy: How can I help?

Jack: I understand that, as you're responsible for the business, you would be responsible for recruitment. Is that correct?
Amy: No, you need to speak with Julie. I'll put you through.

Julie: Hi, who's this?
Jack: Good afternoon, Julie. I've just been speaking to your managing director, Amy Brown, and she suggested I speak to you. She told me that you deal with recruitment.
Julie: That's right, how can I help you?

Julie feels obliged to take the call since it was referred to her by the managing director. Conversely, if Jack speaks to Julie directly, this is what happens:

Jack: I believe that you are responsible for recruitment; is that right?
Julie: That's right, but I don't have time to talk. Just send in your résumé. Thank you.
(She puts the phone down.)

With the larger companies it may be very difficult to get to speak to one of the directors, as they may have no time to take the call. You may have to settle for the recruitment manager, human resources manager or personnel manager. Persistence is the key. Don't give in easily. It is also useful to speak to the person who would gain most from your being in the position you want to apply for. An applicant looking to work as a financial analyst assistant would need to establish contact with the financial analyst. It is the financial analyst who will be most eager to listen. He may well be motivated to take part in the decision-making process when it comes to recruiting if he is impressed.

Here is another example:

Mr. Brown: How can I help you?
Jack: It's Jack Smith, here. Are you responsible for recruiting Office Administrators?
Mr. Brown: No, you need to speak to Leila Patterson.
Jack: Is she available?

Mr. Brown: Hold the line while I transfer you.

Leila: How can I help?
Jack: Hi, Leila. My name's Jack Smith. I've just been speaking with your boss, Mr. Brown, and he suggested that I speak with you. He told me that you are responsible for recruiting office administrators. Is that correct?
Leila: Yes…

One must sound professional and authoritative to get a director's attention. It's all about the power of your voice. The way you speak should be one of your greatest assets. You can use a mobile phone or dictaphone, etc to record and analyse your own voice. Better still, use a voice coach to help you. Practice at improving your telephone manner and vocal tone by role playing. The more enthusiasm you show on the telephone, the greater the likelihood of a successful response.

9. The Telephone Script

Certain statements you give over the phone or at the interview will automatically invite certain kinds of responses, it depends on how the statement is delivered and how the information is perceived.

The following script has been proven to work with remarkable success. It is important to practice it. By memorizing a script you will reflect more confidence than by reading it. Knowing what to say beforehand avoids any possible hesitation in conversation flow. Role playing with a friend or two will prove invaluable.

Follow how Jack uses his script:

Jack: Good afternoon. May I speak with Lisa Moore?

Lisa: Lisa speaking.

Jack: Good afternoon, Lisa. My name's Jack Smith. I'm a graduate in Computer Studies with 6 months commercial experience as a web developer. I recently completed a crash course to further update my skills to today's standards. I am hardworking, punctual and responsible, and actually the reason for my call is to find out whether your company uses the latest technologies?

Lisa: Yes, we do.

Jack: How many web developers does your IT department currently employ?

Lisa: There is an IT manager and two other developers.

Jack: I believe I could enhance your teams' productivity. I was wondering if I could meet you for just ten minutes so that I can explain in a bit more detail how I propose to benefit you and your company. That way, if you do find that you need someone with my experience and abilities in the future, you could consider me. Could you spare ten minutes tomorrow afternoon? (PAUSE)*

Lisa: What time?

Jack: 2 p.m. or would you prefer later?

Lisa: 2 p.m. is fine.

Jack: And may I confirm the address: 14X Luke Street, London W1. Is that right?

Lisa: Right.

Jack: Good, I look forward to seeing you tomorrow afternoon at 2pm. See you then.

*When asking for a time to meet, it is very important to pause for a few seconds at this point. This is because the other person needs a chance to think whether she can fit you in or not. If you don't give her time to think she may be inclined to refuse you.

Customise Jack's conversation to suit your specific situation, but stick to the structure of the script:

- Introduce yourself and give a brief description of your background identifying your strongest skills.

- Seek information that might be helpful to you by asking between three and five questions, but be careful not to give the impression that you are conducting a survey.

- Disclose your intention of looking to enhance the company's productivity sometime in the near future.

- Specify a date and time to meet.

If Jack arranged five such appointments, he would probably get one job offer, in as much as one out of the five companies could be currently recruiting. It's a numbers game. The more employers you meet, the more likelihood you have of meeting an employer who is currently recruiting. You may even convince the employer to create an opening for you.

Here is an example of Anne using her script to get an interview in her favorite Italian Restaurant:

Anne: Good afternoon. Is that Tony, the restaurant manager?

Tony: Speaking.

Anne: Good afternoon Tony, my name's Anne. I have dined at your restaurant on several occasions. I have been impressed with the menu; atmosphere and the service provided by your staff and therefore I have recommended your restaurant to my family and friends.

Tony: Thank you.

Anne: The reason for my call is that I would like to be given an opportunity to join your team. I am hard-working and have relevant work experience, so I was wondering if I could meet you for ten minutes so that I can explain in more detail how you can benefit from my hard work. Could you spare ten minutes tomorrow late afternoon?

Tony: No, but I can see you in the morning when it's not so busy.

Anne initiated the call by speaking positively about the restaurant. This puts the restaurant manager in a more positive frame of mind which subsequently leads to an interview.

Your attitude is important. Sheila told me that she would have no chance in passing her interview next week because of the substantial no. of other applicants. Well, she might just get what she expects! When Jack goes to an interview he expects to get the job; he doesn't care how many other applicants he is up against. If one person can do it, so can you. Jack doesn't think about *how* he will get the job, but *when* he will start the job.

10. Common Objections Over The Telephone

Here's a list of some common telephone objections:

'We have no vacancies at present.'
'I have no time, I'm too busy.'
'Just email your curriculum vitae.'
'We're not looking to recruit till next year.'
'I'm not interested.'
'We don't accept applications over the phone.'
'If I agreed to meet everyone that called me, I wouldn't get any work done.'

It's what you say and how you say it. Sounding positive and confident inspires confidence in others. Someone will only have confidence in you if you show confidence in yourself. Confidence is contagious! Below are some examples of how to deal with each of the listed objections.

'We have no vacancies at present.'
That's fine, but I may be interested in anything that you may have in the future. I'm sure that like a lot of other successful companies you are looking to improve productivity. I need only a few moments of your time. Could you spare just ten minutes tomorrow afternoon, perhaps?

'I have no time, I'm too busy.'
I'm asking for just ten minutes of your time, even if it means meeting you during your coffee break; I'm sure it will be worthwhile. I know a place by your offices that serves one of the best cappuccinos in town; let us meet there and we can talk about improving your department's productivity. I'm sure it would be time well spent. How about the week after next, on Tuesday afternoon, say about 3.30p.m.? Could you pencil me in provisionally, subject to confirmation?
OR *Is there perhaps anyone else I can see?*(Use this question only as a last resort.)

'Just email your curriculum vitae.'

I can do that but I would prefer not to, as it may mislead you. My curriculum vitae focuses on what I've done and not on what I can do. I would much rather show you my curriculum vitae in person so that I can talk through it with you. Although experience can determine ability, I think that one should also judge an applicant by what she can do, not just by what she has already done. By meeting me, you are in a better position to judge my capabilities. (This suggestive statement plants a seed of curiosity in the interviewer's mind.) *Could you spare ten minutes tomorrow morning?*

'We're not looking to recruit till next year.'

That's fine by me. The future is unpredictable. I'd like to meet you anyway, so you can assess my personal qualities and skills and record my details on file. That way, when it is time to recruit, you could get back to me. Could you spare ten minutes tomorrow morning?

'I'm not interested.'

I obviously caught you at a busy moment; I apologise for that. I'll get back to you some other time. Have a good day.

(In this scenario, call back a couple of weeks later with a second attempt.)

'We don't accept applications over the phone.'

The reason for my phone call is to gain as much information as possible on the positions you may have, so that I can make a decision on whether to apply or not. I only apply for jobs that I am suitable for. If its fine by you, I'll drop off my curriculum vitae tomorrow morning; at least then I would know for sure that you had received it. Can you spare five minutes tomorrow morning for a brief meeting?

'If I agreed to meet everyone that called me I wouldn't get any work done.'

Agree to meet me and you will get more work done because my services can result in saving you time and money. You would then have time to meet more people. How about this Wednesday afternoon?

In addition, confirming an appointment by phone should be done preferably a day prior to the appointment date. Assume that the appointment date is mutually convenient; never ask, as this gives the employer more of an option to say 'no'. Instead reveal a good reason for meeting. Following the example below would lead to a successful outcome.

Good afternoon. It's Jack here. We spoke a couple of weeks ago and it was suggested that I call back to remind you that we are meeting tomorrow at 2:30 p.m. literally for 10 minutes, to discuss how I can contribute to the success of your company. (Confirm the address at this point). I look forward to seeing you then.

11. Application Letters

The letter used whenever an employer has asked for a curriculum vitae, often in response to an advertisement, should focus on matching your qualifications to the advertised requirements of the position.

The letter used to contact employers who have not advertised or published job openings should focus on matching your qualifications to the perceived needs of the employer based on your own research and imagination.

Where possible, address the covering letter to a specific person by name and job title. This requires minimal research that will ultimately pay off. When approaching a company that has not advertised any openings, phone the company and ask for the name of the appropriate person, e.g. the recruitment manager, supervisor, or office manager, etc. It will also be useful to ask for their direct telephone number and email address. The letter should usually be no more than three to five paragraphs on one page, and its paper and style should complement that of your résumé or curriculum vitae.

Here is a sample covering letter...

Your address

Date

Michael Hayes
Director
XYZ Ltd
25X Moor Lane
London XX1 XYZ

Dear Mr. Hayes,

Further to a recent call made to your company, and a brief conversation with your receptionist Lisa, I now write outlining how I propose to benefit you and your company.

Last year I graduated in Business Studies at London University. The course enabled me to obtain a sound knowledge in the following areas: marketing, communication and media studies.

My attached curriculum vitae gives brief details of my work experience. During my time at XYZ Travel, I gained invaluable work experience in the travel industry. This experience, coupled with my knowledge and motivation, would make me a valuable member of your team. As it is very difficult to judge someone's potential by their curriculum vitae, I was hoping to arrange a meeting with you sometime so that I could give you a more bigger and complete picture.

I look forward to hearing from you.

Yours sincerely,

Simon Peters

If you are responding to an advertised job, replace the first paragraph of the cover letter, with, for example:

I read with interest the position of trainee marketing assistant advertised in this week's local newspaper …

Once a meeting has been arranged, send a letter or email to confirm it. You are thereby acting professionally.

Dear Mr. Hayes,

Further to our recent conversation, I write to confirm our appointment on 21ˢᵗ March, 2007 at 9:30 a.m.

I look forward to meeting you.

Yours sincerely,

S. Peters

Alternatively, if you find you have no choice but to send your curriculum vitae and covering letter prior to an interview, you don't need to mention this in your follow up call. Assume that the company has already received your curriculum vitae. The following example illustrates the importance of this:

Jack: I sent my curriculum vitae to you and I'm just calling to check that you received it.

Employer: Yes we did, but unfortunately we don't have any vacancies at present. If anything does arise in the future we'll be in touch. Thank you.

Mentioning that you sent your curriculum vitae gives the employer an opportunity to say 'No'. You must stay in control of the conversation. Consider another approach:

Jack: I'm just calling to find out more about your company. Do you have a purchasing department?

Employer: Yes.

Jack: Well, I have good experience in purchasing and I'm looking for a position that can allow me to utilise my skills.

Employer: Do you have experience in …

Here, the employer has received your curriculum vitae, but gets drawn into a conversation. The key is to get the employer to make a decision on your character and abilities, not on your curriculum vitae. By making the assumption that the employer has already seen your curriculum vitae, there is little point in bringing it up at the beginning of the conversation.

The next example is an email response to a job advert for a graphic designer that attracted a lot of attention.

Email Subject: A graphic designer who can deliver results fast.

Dear Sir/Madam,

After reading your advert in my local paper, it immediately seemed to me that you are looking for someone with skills and qualities that closely match mine. If you would like to discuss this further, my contact details are as follows:

Mobile: 0777 XXXX XXX

Email: emily@yahoo.com

Yours faithfully,

E. Richards

This rather short and, perhaps, not too formal letter can be effective because it is unique and hence allows you to stand out from the crowd. It can work better with the smaller companies, but should ideally be followed up with a phone call.

12. Self Marketing

Once Jack acquired the ability to sell, this opened up doors to many other opportunities, new opportunities, as well as existing ones which he wasn't yet aware of. This is because having the ability to sell gives you an advantage when it comes to using your people skills. The company that Jack was with eventually closed down due to the recession. Only two out of the ten sales consultants within this company were making sales. One thing that puzzled Jack, was the fact that these two consultants, Samantha and Tim, were able to sell despite the recession. The fact of the matter was that Samantha and Tim were successful because they remained confident despite the change in economic climate. If you are good at what you do and are able to communicate and demonstrate that fact, then you are on the road to success.

Following is an example of how Jack utilizes his marketing procedures, the principles of which may be used as guidelines for marketing yourself to an employer:

Jack would contact the companies by phone, and then compile a list of potential customers that he felt he could work for. Next he would establish the names of the persons within each company that had the power to recruit. The following shows Jack's typical success rate:

100 phone calls
10 meetings/interviews
2 Job Offers

Ratio 100:10:2
Jack would make the assumption that most companies had openings for him. Jack made an appointment with TTT Ltd. to meet the recruitment manager, Brigitte. When he arrived she wasn't in the most receptive of moods. She had only five minutes to spare and enough staff with his skills. Jack remained positive, though it was difficult under these circumstances. When people around you are negative it can make you feel negative as well. An individual's mood can, to a certain extent, be dictated by his or her surroundings, and so a positive attitude can

rub off on someone else. The meeting went on to last for 20 minutes and ended with a handshake, a smile on Brigitte's face and a job offer for Jack. What does this tell us? It tells us that you cannot prejudge others. A *no* can be converted to a *yes*.

Consider the following:

It would take Jack 2 hours to get one interview over the phone. He worked at it 2 hours a day, 5 days a week. Therefore, he was able to achieve five interviews a week . Jack's friend, Sarah, who was unemployed, was discussing the possibility of getting a job, although she was convinced that it would be difficult to find one. Jack shook his head in a gesture of refusal and said 'But Sarah, it's easier than you think to get a job interview. Think about it!'

Jack is able to get 5 job interviews in one week (one a day).

Apply the same work ethic to your job hunting and it will result in interviews. Spending just one hour a day on the phone to potential employers will guarantee you a minimum of two interviews per week.

Jack believes that the personal approach is key to self-marketing. He sees a job advertised:

"IT sales consultant wanted. Email your cv to info@xyx.co.uk"

Jack finds out XYX's company details from the internet and calls them. He introduces himself as an IT consultant, but doesn't disclose the fact that he saw the advert. This increases his chances of getting the job, as his curriculum vitae will stand out more than those simply sent to the email address given in the advert. By being a confident salesperson, he convinces the employer that he is more than capable of doing the job and hence gets an interview.

Successful job hunters are good sales people. Learn from the examples given about how to market yourself. Learn to be a good sales person and you will make a very good job hunter.

Consider getting a website set up to further market yourself. Your website is your online curriculum vitae which could be accessed by hundreds of potential employers. If you choose to do this, ensure that you have a secure login page setup to restrict access to employers or employment agencies.

If you can't get that interview, consider another one of Jack's tactics:

Jack made a video clip of his presentation which delivered an insight into his background, what he was looking for in the work place and what he could offer. This video clip was then uploaded on the internet and the web address was emailed to the prospective employer. His approach got the employer's attention and finally Jack was able to get the interview he was after.

13. Monitoring Your Progress

Organising yourself includes monitoring your performance at every stage. Closely monitor yourself by keeping track of the number of phone calls made and interviews generated. Success at this stage is defined as getting an interview, and your success rate increases with experience.

Jack's success rate on the telephone was 10% when he first started. It is now 40%. This means that it takes Jack ten telephone conversations with the appropriate contacts to get four interviews. However, it might have taken fifty phone calls to get those ten conversations. (Every so often, the appropriate contact may not be available to take the call.) Fifty phone calls may sound a lot, but if you consider that each phone call need only take a couple of minutes or less, it is possible to conduct all fifty phone calls within two hours. Seen as one interview generated every two hours, Jack's example is made much more plausible.

A list, database or set of index cards organised by 'Call back date' is an efficient way of ordering and monitoring your calls. For example:

Company: XYZ Ltd.
Address: 56 Tree Court, London WXX 4XX
Tel Number: 020 800 XXXX
Contact: The director
12/12/07   The receptionist, Tracy, told me to call back.
13/12/07   The director requested my resume. Call back next Tuesday.

You can use the following codes as shorthand:
CB – call back
NI – not interested
SL – send letter
NA– no answer

Contact companies directly. Approaching employers when you do not know whether or not they are recruiting is essential for the serious job seeker, but never bluntly ask, 'Do you have any vacancies?' Always make the assumption that there is a space for you in any company that you approach. This puts you in a more positive frame of mind, which reflects, in turn, a positive image.

Follow-up and persistence contribute to a successful job search. If you are serious about employment, you must plan your follow-up. Situations change and that employer who is not recruiting today may be looking for someone tomorrow, so the key to successful job hunting is to maintain communication with your contact.

Jack's Plan

9.30 - 10.30: Obtain a list of businesses from the internet or phone book.
10.30 – 12.00: Spend 1.5 hours on the phone to establish contact names.
12.00 – 13.00: Lunch.
13.00 – 13.30: Practice the telephone script and methods of tackling objections with a friend.
13.30 – 15.30: Using your script, book as many interviews as possible over the phone.
15:30 - 16.00: Coffee Break
16.00 –17.30: Prepare for the interviews.

14. The Curriculum Vitae and Application Form

Your curriculum vitae should be either one or two pages long, depending on what you are looking for and your prior experience. Jack knows exactly what he wants and he has the relevant experience, so is therefore better off using a two-paged curriculum vitae. Tom, however, doesn't really know what he wants, and so he should use only one page that displays general information on his positions previously held, but omitting detail. By using this approach the employer doesn't really have enough information to make a decision and would perhaps call him in for an interview in order to get more information. Giving too much detail on your curriculum vitae can set the employer off in the decision making process. Your aim is to whet his appetite.

It is common practice for the employer to initially judge the candidate by his curriculum vitae. The objective is to get the employer to make a decision on the interview, not on the curriculum vitae. It is very important to withhold from showing your curriculum vitae until you are in a position to present it in person. Failing that, if it is practical, visit the company (remember to look professional) and hand over your curriculum vitae to the person responsible for the position or as a last resort to the receptionist. By doing this you have shown that you are keen and confident. If you have been given no choice but to email or send your curriculum vitae in the post then do so, but follow up with a phone call to ensure that your curriculum vitae has fallen into the right hands.

An example of a curriculum vitae of someone with some educational qualifications and commercial experience follows:

CURRICULUM VITAE

Mission Statement: To develop many software applications professionally and to train as many users as possible in these software applications.

PERSONAL DETAILS:

Name:	Gemma Chambers
Address:	Flat 7,
	2XX Fairfax Rd
	Kensington
	London W1 5XX
Tel no:	020 77XX XXXX
Mobile:	07956 XXXXXX
Email:	gem010@yahoo.co.uk
Date of Birth:	27 November 1977
Nationality:	British

EDUCATION:

2006 IT Training Centre, London – Internet for beginners (Part-time) I was nominated Project Team Leader in the development of a website
1997-2001 University of London - BSc (hons) Computer Studies

1994-1996 ABC College, London - 3 'A' Levels
            Mathematics, Science and Psychology

WORK HISTORY:

2006-2007   Computer Programmer, CD Access Ltd
I created computer games and business programs using sophisticated software tools. Working amongst a team of five programmers, I was also responsible for developing test plans and writing technical manuals.

2003-2004   Business Development Manager, AAA Company

I developed marketing strategies for business travel services to London based companies and travelled around the Uk, presenting company services to senior managers. I negotiated deals on behalf of clients and managed existing client accounts.

2002-2003   Telesales Professional, ABC Marketing Group
I marketed products on promotion to company directors in the UK and across the continent. I was involved with setting up and launching advertising campaigns. Utilizing the contact management software, I recorded data for analysis.

1999-2000   Computer Operator, XYZ LTD
My tasks included the daily operation of the computer system and some programming. Maintaining daily and weekly backups of data and training new staff on the system. I completed daily task reports for assessment by management.

SKILLS: Computer literate, fast typist, good time manager and organiser, problem solver, internet marketing.

INTERESTS: Psychology, management techniques, Japanese corporate culture, yoga, kendo, dining out and socialising.

REFEREES: Available on request

A *mission statement* or career objective is a summary of the goals you want the reader to focus on. If you imagine that your curriculum vitae is the front page of a newspaper, then your mission statement is the headline. Only include this section if you are sure of what you want in your career, as it will come up in the interview.

Interests
An interest is not necessarily a hobby. You may for example have an interest in something you don't know much about but are interested to discover more on. It can been seen from Gemma's curriculum vitae that she is interested in kendo, though she has never had a lesson. The

more interests one has, the more interesting one sounds. Include 7 to 10 interests. Establish some interests that might be beneficial to the type of organisation you are applying to. Consider Gemma's interests: Psychology, management techniques, Japanese corporate culture, yoga, kendo, dining out, socialising

Psychology relates to every part of our lives. An interest in *management* can be relevant since many jobs require some sort of management role. Having *Japanese corporate culture* as an interest shows that you are open minded and aware of other work cultures. Including *dining out* is a nice touch as it gives the interviewer scope for extra questions. *Socialising* shows that you enjoy dealing with people and you are perhaps a good listener.

References are a backup; if you can produce a positive image, then the company may not resort to checking them. Employers tend to require two work references. Character references are often not essential but they can be a bonus. Offer to supply three references - two work references and one character reference; it indicates confidence on your part.

Reasons for Leaving
Although this hasn't been included in the example, this may come up in the interview. Look for positive statements about why you left a job such as 'temporary position', 're-organisation of the department', or 'offered a better opportunity elsewhere', etc.

It is important to be truthful in an application. Tell them what they want to hear, but don't be dishonest, simply focus on the positive. If you lack experience or qualifications, you can still word your curriculum vitae to look impressive. For example, your mission statement, skills and interests need to be the focal points, so emphasize these sections in order to outweigh any weaknesses in other sections of your curriculum vitae. What is ultimately important is that you are able to deliver the goods.

Take an extra copy of your curriculum vitae and talk through it positively. Always give a good profile of each company you have worked for.

Here is an example of a curriculum vitae of someone with limited academic qualifications and work experience. Despite these limitations he is still able to produce a reasonable curriculum vitae.

CURRICULUM VITAE

Mission Statement: My goal is to gain experience in the travel and tourism industry, where my true potential can be unlocked. I am responsible, hard working and a fast learner and I have the determination and motivation to succeed.

PERSONAL DETAILS:

Name:	David Piper
Address:	Flat 2
	1x Stockton Road
	London SW20 XXX
Tel no:	020 77XX XXXX
Mobile:	07958 XXXXXX
Email:	david02@hotmail.co.uk
Date of Birth:	02 May 1990
Nationality:	British

EDUCATION:
GCSEs in the following subjects:

English Language
   - General principles of the English language;
Mathematics
   - Arithmetic, graphs, statistics, algebra;
Chemistry
   - Inorganic and organic;
French
   - General conversation and grammar for everyday situations;

Computing
   - Databases, programming, web design

WORK HISTORY:

Part-Time Shop Assistant at XX Clothing Stores (2005- to date)
My duties included the following:
serving customers,
cash-handling,
training new staff,
dealing with customer queries and complaints,
keeping the shop floor clean and tidy,

SKILLS: Telephone skills, customer service, internet skills, good team player, planner, well organised, sales skills, decision maker, fast learner.

SOFTWARE PACKAGES: Windows (all versions), Microsoft Office (Word, Excel, Access, Power Point.)

CLUB MEMBERSHIPS/SOCIETIES: Kamon Martial Arts Federation, local tennis club, Japanese Society.

ACHIEVEMENTS: Employee of the Month, completed London Marathon.

INTERESTS: football, tennis, chess, watching movies, music, dancing, fashion, travel, roller-skating, martial arts, guitar and piano.

REFERENCES: Excellent references available on request.

You will notice that I included some further sections: Software Packages, Club memberships/Societies and Achievements. These act as enhancers to David's curriculum vitae.

Employers may focus on any gaps on your curriculum vitae, so be prepared to give an explanation for any gaps that you may have. An easy way to do this is by placing a blank sheet of A4 along side your curriculum vitae. Next, write out all the periods on this blank sheet that the curriculum vitae doesn't account for, for example:

(Gap) 2004 – 2005: traveled around the world

(Gap) 2005 – 2006: helped family business

If you are a housewife or husband, mention it on your curriculum vitae; cleaning, cooking and looking after children all constitute a job in itself.

Some companies require you to fill out an Employment Application Form. Jack took six hours to complete an application form for a position in Information Technology with a major airline. Most application forms ask similar questions; therefore, Jack found that he was able to use this one as a guide for filling out others. In fact, by using this application form as a template, it would take Jack less than an hour to complete similar application forms. Use as much time and effort as possible to complete your application form and good results will surely follow.

You can refer to your curriculum vitae when completing such forms. Pay particular attention to the following types of requests for information:

- *Give us reasons why you have applied for this position and why you should be selected.*

- *Include here any further information that you think we should be aware of.*

Such questions give you an opportunity to sell yourself, so sell yourself hard, i.e. communicate your strengths. Use them to your advantage and include as much information as possible, giving examples.

The Attribute-Advantage table

The Attribute and Advantage table can be used to structure your answers in application forms and in the interview. Follow the instructions below:

1. Make a two-column list with the first column headed 'Attribute' and the second column headed 'Advantage'.

2. Highlight all the relevant attributes that could be beneficial to the company. List these in the 'Attribute' column.

3. In the 'Advantage' column list the corresponding examples that the employer could benefit from. For example:

Attribute	Advantage
Educated to degree level	Knowledgeable and able to meet deadlines
Fast typist	Ability to input information at fast speeds
Challenger	Not afraid of hard work
Can speak French	Capable of dealing with French clients

Structuring your answers in this way communicates your suitability for the position more effectively.

15. Body language

Your body language can reveal your true personal qualities. Bear in mind the following tips:

- Maintain good eye contact throughout the interview.
- Do not discuss any negative issues, because doing so may induce bad body language.
- See that your appearance expresses motivation and professionalism. Dress as though you want the job, even as if you already have the job. Your appearance is a statement of who you are, so being well groomed is essential. Look successful and you will be successful.

"A picture is worth a thousand words."
The picture you create will greatly influence your chances of being hired. Most employers form a first impression during the first few seconds of a meeting. Use a firm handshake and be aware of your posture (chin up). The clothes you wear can affect your attitude and confidence level. When you take the time to dress for success you will tend to feel good about yourself. We live in a world where image is very important. While image alone will not win the job offer, it will take you a long way toward it. If the job is office-based carry a briefcase or laptop, it gives that final touch of professionalism. Bring a notebook and pen. Look right for the job.

It may be difficult to express your good qualities to, say, a director of the company who walks through the interview room having no time to stop and talk. He will have to judge you by what he saw – your appearance. He may not necessarily take part in the decision making process, but a remark from him, such as, 'She looks as though she will fit in', can make all the difference. Prepare for any possible criticism prior to the interview.

If you look good, you feel good. The primary goal is to 'feel good' about the way you look and so project a positive image. When you feel good about yourself, you naturally convey confidence and a positive attitude. These non-verbal messages are as important in the interview as the verbal skills you use in selling yourself.

16. The Interview

A lot of work goes into a successful job search campaign, and the interview is a critical step toward the goal of employment. If you are consistently being interviewed you should expect job offers. If you are not getting interviews you need to re-evaluate your job search strategy. In other words, if your problem is getting an interview, then there may be a problem with your initial approach, curriculum vitae or application form. If you have problems in passing the interviews, then it may have something to do with your performance at the interviews.

The interview is a sales meeting, and you are both the salesperson and the product - you are selling your services. Basic interview questions can take a variety of forms, but if you have prepared for the interview and are confident in your abilities, none of these questions should be too difficult to answer.

The purpose of an interview is to become acquainted with the interviewer and to learn about one another. The interviewer wants to learn how you might meet the company's needs. However, it is also an opportunity for you to evaluate the company.

Jack spent twenty minutes on the preparation for an interview with a consultancy firm. On a sheet of paper he listed what he could offer the company and he made predictions on what the company could offer him. He also listed his relevant experience and how he would present this verbally. Although he didn't really have enough time to prepare fully or rehearse his presentation, it seemed a lot easier to remember during the interview because he had taken the trouble to write it down.

Present yourself for the interview no more than fifteen minutes early. However, If you are late, remain positive because its never too late to impress the interviewer. When waiting in the reception area, be pleasant to the receptionist. The interview begins as soon as you enter the building. Give a good first impression. Small talk breaks the ice at the beginning of the interview and displays confidence on your part at the end. Therefore, it is essential to use small talk as soon as you are greeted by the interviewer, as well as, after the interview, on your way out of the building.

Be different. Learn to stand out from the crowd, but get noticed for the right reasons. Show that you have potential. Support your answers with examples from your experience.

The interviewer generally follows a structure which one must anticipate in order to gain some control.

An interview usually takes the following stages:

Start Phase

The introductory hand shake followed by small talk.

Main Phase

The interviewer might spend some time describing the company and the position before the questions start.

The questions.

End Phase

Ask questions.
Summarize your strengths.
Close the interview.
Exit: a hand shake followed by small talk.

Most of the above would also apply to a second interview. If the interview is conducted via the telephone, then a good tip would be to prepare by writing down all the questions you anticipate, including your carefully planned answers, which you can refer to.

Think about reasons to succeed, not reasons to fail; try to be 100% confident. If you are not confident, then you cannot expect people around you to have confidence in what you say. If you lack confidence, try to act confident. What matters at the interview stage is that you are able to pass it and your attitude plays an important part in this. If you fail, don't feel bitter; a failure is a step closer to a success. We learn from all of our experiences, whether they are good or bad.

Think about some standard interview questions and how you might respond. Generally, many interview questions from one interview to the next are more or less the same, so you can probably predict most of the questions you are likely to be asked; but don't give predictable answers. Most questions are designed to find out more about you, your qualifications, or to test your reactions in a given situation. If you lack experience or skills in a required area, think about how you might make up for such deficiencies.

17. Key Questions and Model Answers

Please note that the answers given in the following section are not necessarily given by the same candidate. My objective here is to show a variety.

1) Tell me about yourself.

My name's Elaine Foster. I was born in Manchester and decided to move down to the South to study for a degree in Fashion Technology. I graduated last year and I gained ten months' commercial experience in a major fashion outlet during my student placement. I recently completed a crash course that enabled me to update my skills to today's standards. I then went on to work for 123 Hotel Group, one of the largest hotel chains in the world, where I took an active part in assisting the fashion designer in the design of new uniforms for the hotel staff. I am looking for a challenge and I find the fashion industry very challenging.

(Aim to spend about 5 minutes on your answer to the above question and remember to give positive profiles of previous employers.)

2) Why do you want this job?

This position would enable me to use and enhance my skills and experience. The location is perfect. Learning your systems and procedures with the tools and technology you offer at my disposal would realise my full potential. I would get to know your work procedures inside out.

3) Why should we employ you?

I am hardworking, punctual, responsible, loyal, and I am sure that my academic skills, coupled with my past experience, would be of substantial benefit to your company. I also live locally.

(Even if you don't live too close, explicitly stating that the travel will not be a problem eliminates location as a potential problem that can be used against you.)

4) Tell us about your spare time activities?

Dining out in restaurants; I love Japanese, Korean, Chinese, Indian and Italian food. I'm also interested in poetry, animation, reading, music and cooking exotic dishes.

5) What are your weaknesses?

Pick out the weaknesses that can be perceived as strengths and present them positively. For example:

I am too generous. My friends tell me that I work far too hard. I sometimes set my goals too high. I don't accept compliments easily. Perhaps I am too self critical, but I try not to expect too much from other people. I think that the best way to improve performance is to get feedback from colleagues. Really, to me, if the company performs well, everybody wins, so I am not afraid of criticism. Actually, I see it as positive.

6) Why did you decide to switch from music to catering?

I was good at making music, but never in a position that would enable me to get on the property ladder or own a car. I believe that if I diverted the time and energy that I used in my music to a chef role, the financial benefits would increase. I am attracted by a challenge, and that's the reason I like cooking for others.

7) What relevant experience do you have?

I have a wide range of experience, including organizing food for wedding parties and social functions, etc. Moreover, I have the confidence to apply this knowledge and experience.

8) Tell me about the course you studied at University.

The course in Business focused mainly on marketing research, business systems analysis and advertising. I chose to specialise in advertising as I found this to be the most interesting module. My final year project enabled me to put my marketing skills into practice. However, I later discovered that I really wanted to establish my career in the catering industry.

9) What has been your greatest achievement so far?

My greatest achievement was acquiring the ability to sell, the fact I was able to develop this creative ability has opened up a whole range of opportunities for me.

10) Where do you see yourself in five years?

I see myself either managing the company restaurant or setting up new restaurants, in your New York or Tokyo offices, for instance. I want to grow with the company.

Now that you know some of the key questions and are able to give good answers you are half way there. Interviewers need to know why you want the job. You must show that you are interested in *this* job and *this* company, not *any* job in *any* company. Doing so makes the employer feel important.

Anticipate difficult questions at interviews, and if you don't know the answer, rather than replying with something like, *I don't know*, you might say: *That's a question I can't answer right now, but if I successfully answered all the other questions I think I'm not doing too badly. I don't know everything, but I am a fast learner.*

18. Common Interview Objections

Some interviewers can be very direct, i.e. they will be upfront with their reservations. Therefore, in this section there are scenarios and techniques that you can use to help you be more convincing to the interviewer.

Consider the following interview objections:

'We feel that you don't have enough relevant experience.'
'You are under-qualified.'
'You are over-qualified.'
'You don't have enough management experience.'

Lack of relevant experience

Anne and Liz both completed a BA in Journalism. Neither had any work experience, but they managed to obtain jobs in different companies. Both women took on similar jobs as trainee journalists. After one year both women were assessed on their knowledge, skills and experience. These results were compared. It turned out that Liz made a far better journalist than Anne.

The moral of the story is that no two people learn at the same pace, and training procedures tend to differ from company to company. One cannot judge a person on experience alone. A job applicant must be judged not only by what she has done, but what she can do; hence the importance of identifying your skills and motivation.

Lack of qualifications

Jim had a degree in Construction Studies while Alan didn't undertake any further education. Having left education at eighteen to start a career in hotel management, Alan later decided that it was not something he was at ease with. He wanted to switch to a completely new profession: construction. He later managed to get a job as a trainee construction engineer. Jim joined the same company to do the same job. It turned out that although Jim had the academic qualifications in this field, his job performance was not any better than Alan's.

A person who is educated has proved that he is capable of studying and passing exams, whereas a person who is not educated has not proved this. In this case, he would have to prove that his lack of education doesn't necessarily mean that he is incapable of succeeding in education or in a career.

Over-qualified

Being over-qualified still indicates that you are qualified for the job. The point to emphasize here is that you want this job because this is the kind of job that you enjoy and really want to do. And that, by taking on this position, you would increase the company's productivity.

The Expected-Detected Model (ED)

In the job interview, there is an answer for everything. The ED model is that answer. For example, consider the *You don't have enough management experience* interview objection. Using the ED model, one responds,

'My previous boss *expected* me to lack management skills, but when he gave me an opportunity he *detected* that in fact I was capable.'

The ED model can be used to tackle almost any objection. For example, an interviewer may think you live too far away and hence traveling to and from the company would exhaust you. You can use the ED model to tackle this objection successfully:

'In the past I *expected* that location would pose a problem, but when I actually started one of my previous jobs I *detected* that traveling long distances to and from work was something I actually became accustomed to and hence didn't decrease my work performance. In fact, I used the time to familiarize myself with projects and work-related issues.

19. Questions To Ask The Interviewer

During the interview it is good practice to ask questions but save most of them till the end. It is at the end of the interview that the interviewer will usually ask if you have any questions. Be prepared to ask at least ten. The more questions you ask the more interest you show. It may be wise to have the questions written out beforehand in a notebook to which you can refer to at the end of the interview. Of course, some of them may have been answered during the interview, so avoid duplication. A good strategy is to avoid any salary-related questions until you have been offered a job. However, a good answer that has been found to work is the following: 'I would like to earn in the region of £25k per annum; but, job satisfaction is very important to me so I would be willing to negotiate.'

Here are some examples of questions for the interviewer:

- How many staff members are currently employed in the department?
- I believe that those who do overtime are the ones most likely to be promoted. Can I be expected to work overtime?
- If I am successful, when would I be expected to start?
- If I am unsuccessful, could I apply for any positions that may arise in the future?
- Where do the employees go for lunch? *(Not that this is significant to the job applied for, but it adds a personal touch.)*
- How many other branches does the company have?
- How does the company advertise to gain more customers?
- Is the company owner or managing director based here?
- Which computer systems/software does the company use?
- Would you consider taking me on for a one week trial so that I can show you what I am really capable of?

20. Closing The Interview

Close the interview in the same friendly and positive manner in which you started it. The key to passing interviews is not only one's ability to give a good presentation, but also to negotiate and close the sale, i.e. to get a decision at the interview. Don't be afraid to put your foot down to get that decision. Consider the following situation in a fashion store:

Sales assistant: What did you think of the boots you just tried on?
    Customer: Good.
(The customer continues to look around the shop.)

Now compare this with the next situation:

Sales assistant: What did you think of the boots you just tried on?
    Customer: Good.
Sales assistant: Would you like to buy them? They did look good on you.
    Customer: Um… Ok then, why not!

If you don't ask, you will never know for sure. The 'close' must be done in a persuasive but polite and professional manner. Aim to get that positive decision. The following is an example of one way to close the interview:

E.g: "If you consider everything that's been discussed today – my skills, experience, qualifications and personal qualities – do you have any reason to believe that I wouldn't be suitable for this position?"

You have now cornered the interviewer in such a way that he has no choice but to tell you his reservations, if he has any. This is advantageous because it gives you an opportunity to sell yourself harder. This sort of question displays a high-level of courage on your part.

You can use the ED Model here to tackle any issues.

Take care to avoid embarrassing the interviewer. For example, suppose Jack closes the interview like this:

> Jack: So what do you think? Can I start Monday?
> Interview Panel: We have more people to see.

This puts the interview panel in an awkward position; and, as a result, Jack does not receive the answer he was looking for.

Propose to work on a one-day or one-week trial period thereby creating the opportunity to demonstrate what you can do. Once you've got your foot in the door, it's a lot easier to succeed further.

21. Following up the Interview

Reflect on the interview and learn from the experience. Finally, send a thank you letter or email to the interviewer. Every "thank you" is an opportunity to reiterate your qualifications and leave a fresh impression in the mind of the reader. This is your opportunity to make one more impression. Thank you letters should be standard tools in your job search, and should follow a standard business letter format. Always plan your follow-up. If there are multiple people involved, be sure to thank each person. Briefly include any pertinent information you might have failed to mention earlier, and be sure to restate your qualifications or abilities. Write and mail the letter as soon as possible after the encounter – preferably the same day while details are fresh in your mind.

Thank the interviewer for her time, and use the letter as an opportunity to provide more information, or maybe answer a question that was not satisfactorily answered during the interview. For example:

Dear Ms. Lee,

Further to our recent meeting, I would like to take this opportunity to thank you for taking the time to see me.

During the interview you asked me if I was willing to relocate. I have thought about this and I am glad to say that I am willing to relocate; I don't have any vital commitments in my town. Also, I forgot to mention during the interview that I have a good understanding of basic accounting and finance; perhaps you would find this useful.

I look forward to your decision.

Yours sincerely,

S. Foster

Make a phone call to the company to find out the decision. Never wait for the company to call you, even though the interviewer may have said that they would. Also, supposing that the interviewer could not decide between you and another applicant, a phone call displays interest. You are demonstrating that you really want the job, and your phone call could make all the difference.

If you fail the interview, take steps to find out why. For example:

Jack: May I speak with David Turner? (David Turner is the person who interviewed Jack.)
David: How can I help you?
Jack: I received a letter today telling me that I was unsuccessful in last week's interview. I would appreciate it if you could shed some light on the reason for my failure so that I can learn from it and avoid making such a mistake in the future.
David: No problem, I will email you before the end of the day.
Jack: Thank you very much.

Once you are successful in getting the job offer bear in mind that keeping a job is just as challenging. As with getting a job, your attitude is the key.

Consider the following scenario: Each day was exciting for Jack in his new job. He would wake up each morning feeling optimistic and energetic. He would arrive early at the office with his mind preoccupied with the excitement of the day's challenges ahead. We all occasionally have bad days at the office, but Jack combated this by making a list of all the benefits of working for his employer. He pinned this list on his bedroom wall where he would refer to it twice a day, once in the morning and once at night before sleeping. This helped him to remain buoyant and enjoyable to work with.

By being well organized and efficient in his work procedures, and clearly happy with his job, Jack was subsequently rewarded with promotion.

Evaluate your successes and failures. The more you learn from the interviews the easier they will become, and you will certainly become more self-assured.

22. Examples of Interview Dialogues

Although this section illustrates segments of conversation in a given situation, you can use it as a guide for similar interview situations that you might find yourself in.

<u>Scenario A</u>

Jack walked into his local employment centre and saw a job that interested him.

Web designer wanted:
Write to the managing director.

Jack enquired and obtained the company details, but was not given the managing director's name. He was advised to send in his curriculum vitae.

Some employers receive hundreds of curriculum vitaes daily and hence classify a curriculum vitae on its own as junk mail. It ends up amongst the pile of hundreds and is seldom addressed. Jack's curriculum vitae was printed on light blue paper, so it could be more easily accessible from the large pile.

The curriculum vitae really needs to be presented in person. Jack obtains the company's telephone number and then phones the company.

Jack: Good morning, may I know the name of the company director?
Receptionist: Chris.
Jack: Thank you.

(Later on in the day)
Jack: Good afternoon. Chris, please.
Receptionist: Who's calling?
Jack: Jack Smith.

Receptionist: Hold the line. I'll see if he's available.

Chris: Good afternoon.
Jack: Is that Chris?
Chris: Yes, who's this?
Jack: Good afternoon Chris. My name's Jack and I'm calling in connection with the job advertised for a web designer. I'm a computer studies graduate with some commercial experience. I'm hardworking and reliable. I'm looking to use my creative skills and knowledge and I think it could be of mutual benefit if I came in to see you to explain my proposal in detail.
Chris: That should be fine, what time were you thinking?
Jack: 3pm.
Chris: Let me just check my diary; 3 p.m. is okay.
Jack: I look forward to seeing you then.

Points to consider:
Rather than sending in his details, Jack saved a lot of time by approaching the managing director directly by telephone. He was confident enough to put his foot down to get the interview he needed.

Scenario B

Sophie sees a job posted in the classifieds section of the newspaper. Again, applications are to be tendered by curriculum vitae only. She decides to phone the company and retrieves the appropriate company contact details from the internet.

Sophie: Good afternoon. Anita Peters, please.
Receptionist: Who's calling?
Sophie: Sophie Gil.

Anita: How can I help?
Sophie: Good afternoon Anita. It' Sophie Gil here. I understand that you are responsible for the Catering department. Is that correct?
Anita: Yes, that's right.

Sophie: I am looking for a position that would enable me to apply my skills and knowledge. Does your company use the latest catering equipment?

Anita: Yes…

Sophie: Are you based in Westminster?

Points to consider:

Despite the instruction not to call the company, Sophie was able to get Anita's attention and give a good impression, hence Anita was willing to continue to listen. The questions you ask at this stage don't have to be entirely relevant. The idea is to get the conversation going as a means of rapport building.

Scenario C

Interviewer: Why did you leave your last job?

Jack: The previous company that I worked for closed down. If it wasn't for me the company would have stopped trading sooner.

Points to consider:

At this stage, the interviewer doesn't really know if Jack is being honest in his statement, and the curiosity is frustrating him. The only way he can find out is by taking Jack on, which he does. However be careful not to exaggerate your abilities; remember, once you've got that job you want to keep it!

Scenario D

Employer: Why do you think you can do the job?

Sophie: Take a good look at my curriculum vitae; it speaks for itself.

Employer: I can't see any blue-chip companies on your curriculum vitae?

Sophie: Some of my previous employers had blue-chip clients that I had direct contact with.

Employer: Sum yourself up in three words.

Sophie: I'm hardworking, responsible and eager to learn.

Sophie: When will I get to know the result?

Employer: We can't tell you now. We have other applicants to interview and I need to discuss it with my Manager. We'll let you know our decision on Thursday.

The following morning…

Employer: Well done. We've decided to offer you the job. You should be pleased.

Sophie: Thank you.

Employer: You can start next Monday.

Sophie: Excellent ! I look forward to it.

Points to consider:

Sophie's remark about a curriculum vitae that 'speaks for itself' demonstrates a high level of confidence in herself and in the achievements listed in her curriculum vitae.

Scenario E (Recruitment Agency)

Recruitment Consultant: You don't appear to have enough experience for this type of position.

Jack: Just get me the interviews and leave me to worry about succeeding in them. I won't disappoint you.

Points to consider:

Jack knows that by reassuring the recruitment agency that he is more than capable of succeeding at the interview, enhances the agency's motivations towards getting the interviews for him. When using recruitment agencies, build a rapport with your recruitment consultant by calling or emailing her on a regular basis. Sell yourself to her in the same way you would sell yourself to an employer.

23. Some Useful Tips

1. A job is not put on a plate for the taking. Determination and motivation will help you succeed in your job search.

2. The major differences between successful and unsuccessful job hunters are in the way they think, the way they communicate, and the way they go about things.

3. As an individual, your attitude is as important as your experience and qualifications during your job search.

4. Take notice of the qualities of successful job hunters that you know. Establish why they are successful.

5. Try to apply only for the jobs you really want. One tends to be good at what one is interested in. Once you get the job, don't assume that your task is over. You have to make a constant effort to keep the job and progress further.

6. During your interview preparation, look for reasons why you should get the job, not why you shouldn't.

7. New companies tend to start off small, so they are more easily approachable. Approach the director. Directors of smaller companies are generally decision makers in the recruitment stage.

8. Look professional at all times during your job search; you never know whom you might meet.

9. Minimise uncomfortable silences during the interview. Demonstrating that you have a sense of humour by coming out with a joke, can work well in this scenario.

10. Show that you are proud of your past experience and qualifications.

11. The manner in which you do your job hunting can reflect the manner in which you would undertake the job you are seeking.

12. Attempt to give a demonstration of your skills right before the employer's eyes. Show samples of previous work.

13. If the company is unable to afford an additional full-time employee, then offer to work part-time or even as a part-time volunteer to gain some experience. If the job is a job worth doing, it's also worth doing part-time or on a voluntary basis (if your financial circumstances permit it). Better still, take on two part-time jobs.

14. A rejection is one step closer to a success. So, the more rejections you get, the closer you are to being accepted. Take steps to find out why you were rejected.

15. Referrals are like gold dust. Always leave a good impression. You may get recommended to other employers.

16. You may have felt that you were perfect for the job, but the interviewer simply didn't feel you could fit in – a personality clash. It's no one's fault, and, fortunately, it doesn't happen often. The interviewer may have just had a bad day. Don't let it discourage you.

17. Send a letter or email to confirm an interview arranged by the company. After the interview, thank you letters must be sent as soon as possible, reflecting your punctuality.

18. Don't be afraid to re-approach a company that has rejected you in the past. The situation may have changed.

19. Let people know what kind of job you are looking for. Somebody somewhere may give it to you!

20. When calling on an employer, ask for ten minutes only and you will probably get at least half an hour. First impressions last, so make a good one.

21. Being communicative also means being a good listener. Be attentive to what your initial contact or interviewer says, because it may help you market yourself later.

22. Develop your telephone skills, sales skills and presentation skills. These skills are the main components that make a successful job hunter.

24. Summary

- Obtain a list of about 50 companies that you aim to work for.
- Make a phone call to each company to establish the name of the director or someone with the power to recruit.
- Prepare a telephone script and develop your telephone skills.
- Practice the telephone script and answers to the possible telephone objections.
- Remember to sound assertive and authoritative.
- Have an appointment book ready for any interview bookings.
- Aim to spend between one and two hours on the phone a day, and monitor your progress.
- Send a letter or email confirming an interview.
- Be aware of your body language and dress professionally.
- Analyse your curriculum vitae, and prepare an explanation for any gaps.
- Prepare answers for the key interview questions.
- Fill out an Attribute/Advantage table to help structure your answers.
- Remember to communicate the benefits and show a 100% positive disposition.
- Make a list of at least ten questions to ask the interviewer.
- Use the 'close' technique to get a decision at the interview.
- Use the ED model to tackle any objections.
- Send a letter or email thanking the interviewer for their time, and include any further information they might find beneficial.

25. Conclusion

I trust you have found this book useful. Now, simply put what you have learnt into practice and you will see the results, and as your confidence increases, so will the job offers.

The internet is becoming more and more popular. Recruitment agencies, as well as employers' profiles, may be accessed via the web. Take advantage!

We are only human, and there will be times when we feel pessimistic. But people generally prefer to associate themselves with those who are more optimistic and ebullient, and so it is important to be upbeat at all stages of your job search programme.

Uphold this attitude once you have found your ideal job and your employers will know they made the right decision. Although we all have occasional bad days, remember why you wanted that particular job in the first place and remind yourself of all the benefits it has brought you. This will help you in your career trajectory and make your workplace a more enjoyable environment.

I hope you have finished this book feeling confident that you can use the tips provided to make substantial improvements in your job hunting. If you have, and you are optimistic, open-minded, and well organised, it won't be long before you too are in a position to say, "I got a job in 24 hours!"

Happy job hunting!

www.ingramcontent.com/pod-product-compliance
Lightning Source LLC
Chambersburg PA
CBHW022133170526
45157CB00004B/1865